Original title:
Lines of Light

Copyright © 2024 Creative Arts Management OÜ
All rights reserved.

Author: Thor Castlebury
ISBN HARDBACK: 978-9916-88-054-8
ISBN PAPERBACK: 978-9916-88-055-5

The Shimmer of Life's Canvas

Colors blend, a vibrant scene,
Brushstrokes dance, alive, serene.
Moments caught, in hues so bright,
Life's a canvas, bathed in light.

Dreams take flight, on woven threads,
With every shade, a story spreads.
From shadows deep, to radiant peak,
Each painted stroke, a voice to speak.

Nature's palette, rich and wide,
Whispers softly, as worlds collide.
In every swirl, in every dash,
Life's true essence, a vibrant splash.

Through trials faced, and joys embraced,
Every hue, through time's own grace.
In the gallery of our hearts,
The shimmer shines, a work of arts.

The Glow of Tomorrow's Promise

Dawn breaks forth, a golden hue,
Promises whispered, fresh and new.
Hope ignites, in morning's light,
Guiding dreams, through softest night.

The world awakens, shades unfold,
Stories waiting, yet untold.
With each step, we carve our way,
In tomorrow's arms, we long to stay.

Echoes of laughter, skies so clear,
In every moment, love draws near.
Together we rise, hand in hand,
Facing the dawn, a future planned.

Stars will fade, as we embrace,
The glow of hope, in every place.
With every heartbeat, dreams ignite,
Tomorrow shines, forever bright.

The Light that Danced

In the morning's gentle glow,
Sunbeams twirl as soft winds blow.
Each ray flutters, a joyful spree,
Nature's ballet, wild and free.

Through the leaves, they weave and sway,
Chasing shadows, light at play.
Whispers of dawn, a warm embrace,
Life awakens with tender grace.

Reflections on a Shimmering Stream

Beneath the trees, the waters gleam,
Rippling echoes of a dream.
Silvery glints where fish dart by,
Secrets told beneath the sky.

Leaves dance gently on the tide,
Nature's mirror, peace inside.
With every splash, a story's told,
Of timeless tales in water's hold.

Starlit Pathways

Underneath the vast, dark sky,
Stars emerge and softly sigh.
Each twinkle guides us on our way,
A celestial map where dreams can play.

Footsteps trace the ancient ground,
In the quiet, magic's found.
Whispers of the night unfold,
A tapestry of stories told.

The Golden Veil of Daybreak

As night retreats, the light ascends,
A golden veil that never ends.
Across the fields in hues so bright,
Morning greets the world with light.

Birdsong rises, sweet and clear,
Welcoming the dawn so near.
Hope ignites with every ray,
Chasing the shadows of yesterday.

Illuminated Threads

We weave our lives with threads of gold,
Each moment captured, stories told.
In patterns bright, we find our way,
A tapestry of night and day.

With every stitch, a dream takes flight,
Embracing hope, dispelling fright.
The fabric glows with warmth and grace,
In every heart, a sacred space.

Glimmers Beneath the Canopy

Beneath the leaves, a secret sigh,
Where shadows dance and spirits fly.
The whispering winds weave through the trees,
A song of peace, a gentle breeze.

Sunlight dapples on emerald ground,
In this haven, magic's found.
Each step unfolds a story shared,
In nature's arms, we're truly bared.

Radiance in Shadows

In darkness deep, a glow emerges,
A flicker bright as night diverges.
The stars above begin to sing,
A melody that hope can bring.

Shadows hide the whispers true,
But light finds paths for hearts anew.
Through cracks and gaps, it spills and weaves,
In every corner, joy believes.

Threads of Dawn

As dawn awakens with gentle light,
We gather strength to face the fight.
Threads of gold entwine the sky,
Painting dreams as clouds drift by.

In the quiet, possibilities soar,
A canvas fresh, we search for more.
Every sunrise a chance reborn,
With hope renewed, the spirit's worn.

The Glow of a Silent Breeze

Whispers of wind through the trees,
Carrying dreams with such ease.
Moonlight dances on the ground,
Nature's magic all around.

Stars above in quiet night,
Glimmers soft, a gentle light.
Every leaf sways with grace,
In this calm, a warm embrace.

Sparks in the Twilight

Fading light as day departs,
Silhouettes of quiet hearts.
Fiery hues paint the sky,
Nature's canvas, vast and high.

Whispers linger in the air,
Moments caught in gentle care.
Sparks ignite the dusky gloom,
Promises of flowers bloom.

The Veil of Morning Glint

Beneath the veil of morning dew,
Promises of day break through.
Sunrise spills its golden grace,
Waking dreams in every place.

Colors burst as shadows flee,
Nature's song calls out to me.
Petals glisten, fresh and bright,
Inviting all to share the light.

Echoes of Brilliance

In the stillness, echoes play,
Whispers from another day.
Memories dance beneath the stars,
Fading softly, leaving scars.

Light and shadow intertwine,
Moments lost, yet still divine.
Every heartbeat, every sigh,
Brilliance captured, oh so high.

Luminous Whispers

In the night where shadows dwell,
Softly speaks a secret spell.
Gentle glows in every heart,
Guiding souls, a brand new start.

From the depths of silent dreams,
Shimmering with silver beams.
Carried on the evening breeze,
Whispers dance among the trees.

Starlit Pathways

Underneath the endless skies,
Twinkling lights catch wandering eyes.
Every step on starlit ground,
Echoes of the lost are found.

Paths entwined with cosmic grace,
Lead us to a brighter place.
Follow where the shadows play,
Through the night, we find our way.

Flickering Echoes

In the twilight's gentle sigh,
Flickering lights begin to fly.
Moments linger, soft and clear,
Echoes of what once was near.

Through the void, a voice will call,
Whispers caught before the fall.
Every memory held tight,
Guides us through the endless night.

Dawn's Embrace

From the depths of darkened night,
Breaks the dawn with golden light.
Softly warms the waking earth,
Bringing forth a brand new birth.

In that moment, hope takes flight,
Colors dance in sheer delight.
Every heartbeat, fresh and free,
Dawn's embrace, a melody.

Dancing Specks

In the air, they twirl and weave,
Tiny dancers, light as leaves.
Sparkling dreams in morning sun,
A silent dance, where all is fun.

They swirl near flowers, kiss the breeze,
Whisper secrets with such ease.
Nature's jewels in glowing flight,
Each one glimmers, pure delight.

As sunset paints the world in gold,
These magic specks, brave and bold.
They fade and shift, then reappear,
A fleeting dance, forever dear.

When Light Meets the Water

Rippling waves, a soft embrace,
Light kisses water, finds its place.
Glimmers dance, a silver sheen,
Nature's canvas, pure and keen.

The sun dips low, the colors blend,
A tranquil sigh, as day will end.
Reflections whisper tales anew,
Of skies painted in shades of blue.

Each drop sparkles, a fleeting dream,
Rippling voices in a gleam.
When light meets water, magic flows,
A symphony of nature's prose.

The Art of Illuminations

Candles flicker, shadows play,
The room awash in soft array.
In this glow, stories unfold,
Of secrets whispered, truths retold.

Dancing flames with colors bright,
Paint the walls in warm twilight.
Every corner comes to life,
In the midst of gentle strife.

Crafted moments, pure delight,
Art of shadows, born of light.
In this dance, we find our way,
Illuminations guide our play.

Fragments of Brilliance

Scattered diamonds on the floor,
Each one tells a tale of yore.
Fragments of brilliance, shining bright,
Whispers of stars found every night.

Tiny pieces of a grand design,
Collecting dreams, both yours and mine.
Like stolen moments, frozen time,
In their gleam, we find the rhyme.

Every glint, a path to trace,
Leading us to a sacred place.
In their dance, the world stands still,
Fragments of brilliance, hearts to fill.

Celestial Murmurs

In the stillness of the night,
Stars whisper secrets bright.
Moonlight bathes the earth in peace,
A soft glow that will never cease.

Dreamers gaze into the sky,
Wondering where the echoes lie.
Galaxies in endless dance,
Inviting all to take a chance.

Comets streak with fervent grace,
Tracing paths across the space.
Each twinkle tells a tale anew,
Of hopes and dreams that dare to brew.

In solitude, the heart will soar,
Through celestial realms that endlessly implore.
With each murmur, we are reminded,
Of the magic that we've all forgotten.

Veins of Radiance

Through the forest, light cascades,
Painting shadows, soft parades.
Branches sway with gentle ease,
Carrying whispers on the breeze.

Golden threads weave through the green,
In a tapestry rarely seen.
Nature's pulse, a vibrant song,
Echoes where the hearts belong.

In the twilight, colors blend,
A radiant force that will not end.
Every petal, every tree,
Holds a story, wild and free.

As the sun dips low and shy,
The horizon embraces the sky.
In veins of radiance, we find,
The beauty of the world entwined.

Chasing the Glimmer

Across the fields, the fireflies roam,
Guiding lost souls back to home.
Each flicker a promise of delight,
Chasing the glimmer deep in the night.

Beneath the stars, dreams take flight,
Casting shadows that ignite.
With every moment, hearts unite,
Caught in the magic, pure and bright.

Eyes wide open, we pursue,
The shimmer of a world so true.
In the silence, we hear the call,
Of glimmers that can hold us all.

In the chase, we find our way,
With every glance, hearts start to play.
Together we weave a story bold,
Of chasing glimmers, ages old.

Sparks Across the Canvas

Brushed with colors, wild and free,
Art unfolds like poetry.
Each stroke a feeling, every shade,
An expression that will never fade.

In the chaos, beauty thrives,
Where imagination comes alive.
Sparks ignite with every move,
Creating wonders that will soothe.

From darkest hues to brightest light,
A tapestry woven, bold and bright.
Each canvas tells a tale unique,
With sparks that dance and softly speak.

As visions come to life and bloom,
In the studio, there's no room.
For doubt to linger, nor for fears,
Just sparks of passion through the years.

The Embrace of Warm Radiance

In the sun's gentle gaze, we bask,
Warmth wrapping 'round, a loving task.
Hearts intertwined in a soft glow,
Together we thrive, letting love flow.

In golden hues, our dreams take flight,
Each moment shared, a rare delight.
With laughter echoing in the air,
The world seems still, beyond compare.

As shadows fade, in twilight's grace,
We find our solace, a sacred space.
Holding on tight, we face the day,
In warm radiance, come what may.

With every dawn that breaks anew,
Our spirits soar, forever true.
The embrace of warmth, a cherished art,
In the light of love, we'll never part.

Echoes in the Dappled Light

Through leaves that dance in gentle breeze,
Shadows play tricks, bringing us ease.
Whispers of nature fill the air,
Echoes of laughter, stories we share.

Beneath the branches, our secrets spill,
Memories captured on time's bright hill.
In every ray that filters down,
The beauty of life, a timeless crown.

As sunlight filters in patterns bright,
We trace our steps in the fading light.
With every rustle, the world awakes,
In dappled glades, our spirit breaks.

In the warmth of dusk, we linger still,
Grateful for moments that time can't kill.
Echoes of joy in the soft twilight,
Dancing in harmony, hearts so light.

The Pathway of Glowing Moments

In the twilight, where dreams commence,
We walk a path, a journey immense.
Each glowing moment, a sparkle bright,
Guiding our souls through the night.

With hands held tight, we chase the stars,
Finding beauty in the quiet scars.
Footsteps whisper tales of past,
In the sacred stillness, finding peace at last.

Time unfolds like petals soft,
Carrying wishes high aloft.
Every heartbeat, a note of song,
In this glowing moment, we belong.

As dawn approaches, we pause to see,
The pathway ahead, where we are free.
Glowing moments wrap us tight,
In this journey shared, love is our light.

Twilight Serenade

In twilight's embrace, the stars ignite,
Melodies linger, a soft delight.
Nature hums its gentle tune,
As day whispers farewell to the moon.

Silhouettes dance upon the lake,
Reflecting dreams we dare to make.
In this serenade, hearts entwine,
With every note, our spirits shine.

The cool breeze carries sweet refrains,
Of love and hope that gently reigns.
Under the sky painted in hues,
We find our solace, forever true.

As night descends like a tender shroud,
We listen close, our hearts so loud.
In twilight's arms, we serenade,
A love that blooms, never to fade.

The Radiance of a Hidden Path

In the silence of the woods,
Whispers guide the wayward souls.
Through shadows deep and glimmers bright,
A secret path of timeless goals.

Leaves shimmer in the soft-lit haze,
Every step carries a gentle glow.
Nature's breath in quiet praise,
Invites the heart to dare and go.

Let the branches part with grace,
Revealing dreams in woven light.
The hidden path, an embrace,
Of magic, wonder, and delight.

Twilight's Embrace

Beneath the cloak of fading day,
The sun dips low with tender sighs.
Stars awaken in soft ballet,
As night unfolds its velvet skies.

Shadows dance in gentle play,
Crickets sing a lullaby.
The world exhales, and dreams convey,
A whisper of the night's sly eye.

With every brush of twilight's hand,
Possibilities in silence bloom.
In this realm, we take a stand,
To weave our tales beyond the gloom.

An Aura of Distant Dreams

In the realm where visions soar,
Past the hills of hope and fear.
Echoes of what we long for,
Guiding us, forever near.

Winds carry whispers from afar,
Stories woven with silver thread.
Stars are scattered like memories,
In the tapestry of the unsaid.

Let every heartbeat mirror light,
As dreams awaken from their sleep.
In the stillness of the night,
We find the treasures that we keep.

Luminescence from Within

Amidst the darkness, a spark ignites,
Awakening the soul's sweet fire.
From depths of silence, hope takes flight,
As the heart's rhythm climbs ever higher.

Dancing embers weave their tale,
Flames of passion, joy, and pain.
In the stillness, love prevails,
A beacon shining through the rain.

Trust the light that burns inside,
For shadows vanish with its grace.
In every heartbeat, dreams collide,
Creating magic in this space.

The Quiet Blaze of Serenity

In stillness lies a quiet flame,
Its whispers soothe, no need for name.
Beneath the stars, the heart finds peace,
Where all the worries slowly cease.

The night embraces, soft and calm,
A gentle touch, a healing balm.
In shadows deep, the spirit soars,
Through tranquil realms, it endlessly explores.

A flicker glows within the mind,
In silence, the answers we can find.
With each breath, a soft release,
The quiet blaze, our inner peace.

As dawn approaches, colors blend,
The quiet blaze will rise, transcend.
In every heart, a spark remains,
Serenity in life's refrains.

Awakened by Starlight

Under the gaze of twinkling skies,
Dreams unfold, as darkness flies.
A tapestry of light so bright,
Awakens souls in the cool of night.

Whispers of cosmos call us near,
Each star a song for those who hear.
With every twinkle, hope ignites,
Chasing shadows, embracing heights.

The moon drapes silver on the ground,
In this realm, peace can be found.
Together, hearts dance in the glow,
Awakened by starlight, spirits flow.

As dawn approaches, shadows flee,
In starlit dreams, we find the key.
To harness light, let spirits rise,
Awakened souls beneath vast skies.

A Cascade of Reflective Dreams

In quiet moments, visions gleam,
A cascade flows, the heart's soft theme.
Ripples of thought, like water's grace,
  Reflecting truths we often chase.

Each droplet carries tales untold,
Of wishes whispered, of hearts bold.
Like autumn leaves that dance and spin,
  They swirl together, deep within.

The night unfolds its secret streams,
Carving pathways through our dreams.
Each shimmering wave, a silent call,
  To seek the beauty within it all.

Through reflective pools, let visions glide,
A journey inward, where joy resides.
In a cascade of hearts, we find our way,
  Creating night from break of day.

Dawn's Gentle Fingerprints

As light creeps in with tender grace,
Dawn paints the world in soft embrace.
With every hue, shadows retreat,
A symphony of day, bittersweet.

The whispers of night begin to fade,
In golden strokes, new paths are laid.
Gentle fingerprints of morning's kiss,
Awaken dreams in a joyful bliss.

Birds sing sweetly, a call to rise,
Their melodies dance with the clear skies.
In every corner, hope is reborn,
With dawn's gentle light, a new morn.

As day unfolds with vibrant hues,
We cherish moments, old and new.
For in each dawn, a promise glows,
Dawn's gentle fingerprints, life bestows.

A Tapestry of Illuminated Hearts

In shadows deep, our spirits weave,
Threads of hope, we dare believe.
Colors blend, like dreams in flight,
A tapestry spun of purest light.

Each heart a stitch in this grand design,
Emotions flow, like rivers divine.
Through joy and strife, we find our way,
Illuminated hearts, forever stay.

The Luminous Dance of Time

Time waltzes softly, a fleeting grace,
Moments whisper, a tender trace.
Stars align in the velvet night,
Each tick a heartbeat, a spark of light.

We sway to the rhythm of day and dusk,
With every breath, the world we trust.
Through ages past, futures yet to come,
In luminous dance, our souls become.

Glowing Embers of Yesterday

Flickering memories, softly aglow,
Whispers of laughter, in twilight's flow.
Stories linger, like embers bright,
Illuminating shadows, soft and light.

Through the haze of time, we reflect,
Warmth of the past, in every aspect.
In dreams we hold, those moments dear,
Glowing embers, forever near.

The Radiant Tapestry of Life

Woven together, our tales unfold,
Threads of courage, in colors bold.
In every heartbeat, a story ignites,
The radiant tapestry, of days and nights.

Joy and sorrow, the fibers entwined,
Each stitch a memory, perfectly lined.
Through trials faced, and triumphs earned,
The tapestry of life, forever learned.

Shards of Hope

In the shadows, a glimmer shines,
Flickers of dreams, in tangled vines.
A heart that beats with fervent grace,
Finds its way in the darkest place.

Through the cracks, the light will pour,
Every fragment holds tales of yore.
With gentle hands, we gather near,
Each shard ignites the flame of cheer.

No storm too fierce to break our will,
Together strong, we climb each hill.
In every trial, a lesson blooms,
From shattered pieces, new life looms.

So lift your eyes to skies above,
Embrace the shards, and share the love.
In every heart, a beacon glows,
From broken paths, true courage grows.

Serenity in the Dawn

Soft whispers dance upon the grass,
As morning breaks, the shadows pass.
The world awakens, bathed in light,
A gentle hush before the flight.

Birds take wing, with songs so sweet,
Nature stirs, and hearts will meet.
A tranquil breeze, a soothing balm,
In dawn's embrace, the soul feels calm.

Golden rays cascade like streams,
Illuminating tender dreams.
Each moment sparkles, pure and bright,
Serenity wraps the day so tight.

So hold this peace, let worries fade,
In dawn's soft glow, we are remade.
With open hearts, we greet anew,
The promise of all that we can do.

The Whisper of Radiant Tides

Oceans stretch, a vast expanse,
With murmurs soft, they sing and dance.
Each wave a tale, a secret shared,
In the depths, the soul is bared.

Moonlit paths upon the sea,
Guiding lost hearts, wild and free.
The whispering tides call us near,
Awakening hopes, calming fear.

In every ebb, a lesson flows,
In every crest, new courage grows.
The rhythm strong, the hearts entwined,
In nature's voice, peace we find.

So listen close, let spirits soar,
Embrace the tide, and seek the shore.
With each whisper, a promise sign,
Radiance waits, in the divine.

Colors of an Uplifted Spirit

Painted skies at twilight's breath,
A canvas rich, defying death.
With every hue, a story spun,
Of battles fought and victories won.

Through scarlet dreams and sapphire tears,
We dance with joy, dismissing fears.
Emerald greens of hope arise,
In gilded moments, love never dies.

Each brushstroke speaks of battles hard,
Of triumphs gained and hearts unmarred.
In every shade, a spark ignites,
Reflecting the strength of our inner lights.

So wear these colors, bold and bright,
Let your spirit shine with every light.
In art, in life, find your reprieve,
In vibrant tones, we choose to believe.

Shimmers of Hope

In the darkness, small lights gleam,
Whispers of dreams in the night's seam.
Hearts alight with quiet grace,
Hope's soft touch, a warm embrace.

Through shadows cast, they gently sway,
Guiding souls along the way.
Each flicker tells a story bold,
Of courage born and love retold.

Rays of dawn break through despair,
Every struggle left to bear.
As fate unfolds with each new breath,
We find our strength, beyond the death.

Hand in hand, we share the light,
Together weaving dreams in sight.
United, we will stand and cope,
For in our hearts, there shimmers hope.

Illuminated Journeys

Across the sea of time we sail,
With winds of change, we will prevail.
Stars above, our guiding quest,
Every moment, life's bequest.

Footsteps echo on the shore,
As dreams ignite, we long for more.
Paths illuminated by the sun,
Where every struggle's just begun.

Mountains high, we climb with zeal,
Each new horizon, fate's appeal.
With every turn, a story spun,
In the dance of life, we become one.

Brighter worlds in every stride,
Journey shared, with hearts open wide.
Through storms and calm, we earn our grace,
Illuminated journeys, time can't erase.

The Glow Within

Deep inside, a fire glows,
In silence, every heartbeat knows.
From ashes rise, a spark so bright,
Illuminating the depth of night.

Embers dance in shadows cast,
Whispers of the future, deep and vast.
With every challenge, we ignite,
The glow within, our purest light.

Voices soft, yet strong and true,
In unity, we find our crew.
Together facing darkened skies,
With inner light that never dies.

So let it shine, the glow within,
Unfolding wings so we can win.
Through every trial, we stand tall,
In the end, we will not fall.

Reflections of Brilliance

In quiet pools, the stars reside,
Mirrored dreams where hopes abide.
Softly glimmering, tales unwind,
Reflections of brilliance, intertwined.

Golden moments, stitched with care,
Echoing laughter fills the air.
With every glance, a story shared,
In the light, we are all bared.

Waves of time, they rise and fall,
Carving memories, big and small.
Capturing joy, love's gentle thrill,
With every heartbeat, time stands still.

So cherish the light that you behold,
In reflections of brilliance, be bold.
For in each moment, rich and rare,
Shines a tapestry beyond compare.

Whispers of the Radiant

In shadows cast by twilight's reach,
Soft murmurs dance along the beach.
They speak of dreams where spirits play,
In golden hues of waning day.

A glimmer hints at hidden paths,
Where twilight's whispers weave their math.
Amidst the light, we seek the sound,
Of every secret love we've found.

With each soft breeze, the echoes swell,
In tales that only time can tell.
The radiant calls from realms unknown,
A melody, our hearts have grown.

So let us linger, hear the truth,
In whispers bright as fleeting youth.
For in each moment, dreams ignite,
Awakening a world of light.

Beneath a Canopy of Glow

Beneath the stars, a fervent night,
The sky unfolds a dance of light.
Each twinkling gem a story speaks,
A universe that dreams and seeks.

The branches weave a cloak of grace,
In moonlit whispers, soft embrace.
We gather close, our spirits twine,
In nature's glow, our hearts align.

With every breath, the magic swells,
As time stands still, and silence dwells.
In harmony, we blend and flow,
Together strong, beneath the glow.

Awake, alive, in radiant hue,
We share the night, just me and you.
Bound by the light, our souls take flight,
In love's sweet glow, we own the night.

Ethereal Traces

Through misty realms where shadows play,
Ethereal traces guide the way.
A whisper lingers in the air,
As if the night itself is bare.

Footsteps light on paths unseen,
In silken threads of what has been.
Each echo holds a tale divine,
In timeless dance, forever twine.

The distant stars weave stories old,
Of dreams and hopes yet to unfold.
In gleaming sparks, our thoughts take flight,
Carried on winds of velvet night.

So let us chase those fleeting signs,
With open hearts, where magic shines.
For in the traces left behind,
The essence of our souls we find.

Embracing the Spark

In the stillness, a flicker glows,
A fire ignites where passion flows.
With every heartbeat, we draw near,
Embracing sparks that disappear.

The warmth of hope, a glowing flame,
In whispered words, we stake our claim.
With open hands, we catch the light,
In shadows' dance, we take our flight.

Through winding paths and swirling dreams,
We chase the truth in silvery beams.
For in the dark, we learn to see,
The beauty in our destiny.

So let the spark become our guide,
In love's embrace, we will abide.
For in this flame, we are alive,
In every moment, we can thrive.

Fading Hues of Dusk

The sky melts into soft hues,
Whispers of day begin to lose.
Clouds drift like thoughts, slowly fade,
Night's embrace is gently laid.

Stars awaken in silent grace,
Casting dreams in their vast space.
Moonlight spills like silver wine,
Across the canvas, pure divine.

Silhouettes of trees stand tall,
Guardians of twilight's call.
Nature holds her breath to sigh,
As day bids a soft goodbye.

The Warmth of Hidden Horizons

In shadows cast by setting suns,
The warmth of secrets gently runs.
Mountains cradle the fading light,
Embracing all within their sight.

Whispers linger on the breeze,
Carrying tales from distant seas.
Every hue a story spun,
In the glow of the hidden sun.

Fields of gold, beneath the sky,
They stretch as far as dreams can fly.
Moments caught in twilight's hands,
Weaving threads through timeless sands.

The Dance of Elysian Rays

Beneath the boughs where shadows play,
Elysian rays will find their way.
Dancing lightly on the ground,
In their glow, sweet joys abound.

Petals blush as sunlight beams,
Life awakens, stirring dreams.
Each beam a note in nature's song,
Unfolding where our hearts belong.

In this realm of sacred light,
Hope ignites the darkest night.
We join the dance, a gentle sway,
Living fully, come what may.

Shimmering Dreams Unfold

At dawn's approach, the world ignites,
Shimmering dreams take graceful flights.
Each moment a delicate thread,
Woven softly, joy widespread.

Golden rays cast shadows long,
In their warmth, we find our song.
Every heartbeat, a step toward,
The dreams we cherish, our reward.

As night descends, we still embrace,
The magic held in time and space.
For every wish that sparks the soul,
Is a journey that makes us whole.

Glows of Forgotten Memories

In corners of my mind they dwell,
Faded whispers, soft as a shell.
Each moment a flicker, a glimmering light,
Dancing shadows in the heart of night.

Time drifts slowly, like leaves on a stream,
A tapestry woven from a forgotten dream.
Echoes of laughter, sweet and so clear,
Remind me of moments when you were near.

Through dusty pages, stories unfold,
Of vivid adventures, both brave and bold.
Fragmented tales that linger and weave,
A glow of remembrance that never leaves.

Each sigh of the past is a soft, gentle song,
Guiding me back where the heart feels strong.
In the quiet, they spark and ignite,
Those glows of memories, eternally bright.

The Sparkling Embrace of Evening

As the sun dips low, the sky starts to blush,
The world whispers softly in a gentle hush.
Starry glitter dances with the night breeze,
Wrapped in the velvet of twilight's tease.

Mountains stand tall, kissed by the glow,
While rivers reflect all the secrets they know.
Night's soft embrace, a tranquil affair,
Holding our dreams in the twilight air.

Fireflies twinkle like wishes on flight,
In the stillness that follows the fading light.
Together, we wander down pathways unknown,
In the sparkling embrace, we are never alone.

In this moment, time seems to stand still,
A canvas of colors, a heart that can fill.
With each breath, the evening unfolds,
A treasure of stories waiting to be told.

Horizons Aglow

Where the sky kisses earth, a promise divine,
Horizon aglow, colors intertwine.
A symphony painted in amber and rose,
Awakening dreams, as the morning light glows.

Mountains emerge from the misty embrace,
Each peak a story, each curve a trace.
Nature's brush strokes on the canvas so wide,
Inviting the wanderer, who longs for a ride.

A journey begins at the break of new dawn,
With horizons aglow, we are swiftly drawn.
In whispers of wind, the world starts to sing,
A tale of adventure that each heart can bring.

Beyond the horizons, where dreams take their flight,
In the warmth of the day, we chase the soft light.
Hand in hand, we traverse life's vast show,
With the promise of hope in horizons aglow.

The Luster of Lost Wishes

In the quiet of night, wishes concealed,
Glimmer softly, though time may have healed.
Each star a yearning, a desire untold,
Shining like secrets from a past we uphold.

Whispers of dreams that once soared so high,
Drift through the darkness, like birds in the sky.
The luster of wishes, though fragile as glass,
Holds the light of the futures that never came to pass.

In shadows of silence, they linger and sigh,
Woven in stardust, their echoes won't die.
Each flicker of hope, a reminder so sweet,
That lost wishes linger, though life may be fleet.

Yet in the stillness, they shimmer and dance,
In the heart of the night, they offer a chance.
For every lost wish holds a glinting truth,
The luster of dreams is the heart of our youth.

The Winged Dance of Sunbeams

Golden rays play on the waves,
A ballet of light weaves and sways.
Each flicker tells a tale of day,
Nature's brush in bright array.

Whispers of warmth upon the ground,
Laughter of colors, joy unbound.
In gentle flight, the spirits glide,
As sunbeams dance with graceful pride.

Morning dew in soft embrace,
Reflects the beauty, fills the space.
With every flick, a story spun,
In the golden glow, we become one.

The sky ignites, horizons blaze,
In the midst of this sunlit phase.
The winged dance beneath the dome,
In sunlit dreams, we find our home.

The Silhouetted Mirage

In twilight's cloak, the shadows grow,
Whispers of night begin to flow.
Figures loom in the fading light,
A dance of dreams in dimming sight.

Stretched silhouettes on the wall,
Echoing secrets, a silent call.
The air is thick with tales untold,
In this mirage, we lose our hold.

As stars awaken, the night ascends,
The world transforms, time seldom bends.
Each shadow moves, a fleeting grace,
In the twilight's heart, we find our place.

A canvas painted with fears and hopes,
A labyrinth where reality copes.
In the shadows, we search for truth,
The mirrored whispers of ancient youth.

When Shadows Speak in Light

Beneath the glow of moonlit beams,
The shadows gather, weaving dreams.
Soft murmurs echo in the night,
When shadows speak, they reveal light.

Each flicker dances on the floor,
A gentle touch, a whispered lore.
In silence, wisdom drapes the air,
With every shadow, a hidden prayer.

Moments pause, the world breathes deep,
As twilight guards the secrets we keep.
In every hue, a story waits,
When shadows speak, the heart resonates.

Through the silence, our souls collide,
In the embrace of night, we confide.
Their tales entwined, like stars above,
In shadows' whispers, we find love.

Echoes of Light and Shadow

In twilight's arms, the echoes play,
A tapestry of night and day.
Flickering whispers of light's soft grace,
In shadow's depth, we find our place.

Reflections dance on mirrored streams,
Merging worlds of hopes and dreams.
Each step we take in the soft glow,
In echoes, secret paths we sow.

The interplay of dark and bright,
Crafts a canvas of pure delight.
In every flicker, stories blend,
As echoes of light and shadow mend.

With every breath, we draw the line,
Between the dim and the divine.
In this union, we are found,
Echoes of life's resounding sound.

When Light Finds Its Way

In the dawn's embrace, shadows flee,
Gentle whispers dance, wild and free.
Golden rays spill on silent streams,
Awakening the world from dreams.

Fingers of light trace the hills,
Filling the air with radiant thrills.
Nature's palette, rich and bright,
Colors bloom in morning's light.

Each moment glows, a fleeting spark,
Painting landscapes, bright and stark.
Hope ignites in every heart,
When light finds its way, we are part.

The Mystery of Morning Glimmers

Veils of mist cling to the ground,
Hidden secrets waiting to be found.
Softly, whispers call the sun,
As the dance of day has begun.

Glimmers flicker on dew-kissed leaves,
Nature sighs as the soft wind weaves.
Each sparkle tells a story new,
Of miracles in the morning dew.

In the quiet, time seems to pause,
Witnessing creation's timeless laws.
Each breath a promise, fresh and bright,
In the mystery of morning light.

Threads of Cosmic Light

Stars are woven in a tapestry,
Threads of light for all to see.
Across the night, they sing their song,
Binding the universe, vast and strong.

Galaxies swirl in a dance divine,
A cosmic rhythm, fate's design.
Each twinkle glows with tales untold,
Mysteries of the universe unfold.

Fingers of stardust touch the sky,
Dreams of explorers who dare to fly.
In the vastness, we search for clues,
Threads of light lead us through the blues.

Flickering Joys

In laughter's glow, joy takes its flight,
Flickering like candles in the night.
Moments captured, tender and bright,
Each heartbeat a spark, pure delight.

In shared whispers, stories unfold,
Warmth of memories, riches untold.
Every smile a flicker, bright and clear,
Binding us close, ever so dear.

Through gentle storms and skies of gray,
Flickering joys guide us each day.
In the dance of life, we find our way,
Shimmering sparks in the light's ballet.

The Enigma of Soft Radiance

In shadows where whispers play,
Gentle light begins to sway.
Hidden truths, a soft embrace,
A fleeting glimpse of cosmic grace.

The heartbeats of the night unfold,
Stories in whispers, yet untold.
As stardust dances in the air,
Time stands still, an endless stare.

Mirrored thoughts in twilight's glow,
Secrets of worlds we may not know.
A flicker here, a shimmer there,
The enigma lingers everywhere.

In quiet moments, the mind will roam,
Finding solace in the unknown.
With every breath, embrace the light,
Soft radiance, a guiding sight.

Resplendent Journeys

Beneath the skies of azure hue,
We wander paths both old and new.
Each step a tale, a story spun,
Resplendent journeys just begun.

Through valleys deep and mountains high,
We chase the dreams that breathe and fly.
Guided by the stars above,
Each moment wrapped in endless love.

With every sunset's fiery blaze,
We weave our thoughts in twilight's gaze.
Adventures call in sweet refrain,
Together we shall dance in rain.

As dawn appears, a fresh new day,
We'll map our course along the way.
Resplendent hearts, forever free,
In this vast world, just you and me.

The Glow of a Thousand Stars

In a tapestry of night, they gleam,
A thousand stars, a silver dream.
Each twinkle holds a tale so bright,
Whispers of the cosmic light.

From distant realms, they've traveled far,
Guiding souls like a guiding star.
In realms beyond our earthly grasp,
In their glow, the heart will clasp.

With every flicker, stories blend,
A dance of light that knows no end.
They sing of hope, they sing of fate,
In their embrace, we contemplate.

In midnight's arms, we find our dreams,
A symphony of celestial beams.
The glow of a thousand stars above,
Reminds us all of boundless love.

Quicksilver Constellations

In skies where dreams and wishes meet,
Quicksilver glimmers weave and fleet.
Patterns drawn in ethereal thread,
Whispers of the night, softly spread.

Emerald paths and sapphire trails,
Within the starry sea, our sails.
Adventurers in the cosmic flow,
Tracing maps where only stars go.

Moments captured in silken light,
A fleeting dance in the heart of night.
Guided by the heavens' song,
Quicksilver paths where we belong.

As dawn approaches, shadows fade,
The constellations, memories made.
Cradled in the glow of night's grace,
In quicksilver dreams, we find our place.

Hues of the Horizon

The sky blushes at dawn's tender call,
Whispers of gold through shadows that fall.
Deep purples fade into soft morning light,
As day stretches wide, chasing away the night.

Waves of orange dance on the gentle sea,
Each ripple a brushstroke, wild and free.
Clouds adorned with silver, drifting above,
Nature's palette sings with colors we love.

The horizon whispers stories untold,
Of sunsets ablaze, and dreams yet bold.
As twilight embraces, the sky turns to flame,
In the canvas of evening, we find love's name.

With stars that shimmer, our hearts intertwine,
In the hues of the horizon, our souls align.

A Tapestry of Glints

Beneath the vast expanse of night,
Stars weave together, pure delight.
They twinkle softly, a distant grace,
A tapestry of glints, in silent space.

Moonlight drapes like a silver thread,
Embroidered dreams that softly spread.
Each shimmering gem tells tales of old,
Of secrets whispered and hearts bold.

Wonders glisten on a tranquil lake,
Reflecting wishes that we dare to make.
In this embrace of glimmering sights,
We find our solace beneath celestial lights.

A dance of shadows and shimmering beams,
In every flicker, the heart gently dreams.
In this tapestry woven so fine,
We glimpse our hopes in every line.

Beaconing Heartbeats

In the stillness where whispers reside,
Heartbeat echoes, where love cannot hide.
With every thump, a promise is clear,
Guiding us onward, ever near.

Each pulse a beacon in the dark night,
Drawing close those who seek the light.
The rhythm of life in a tender embrace,
Two souls united in this sacred space.

Through valleys of shadows and peaks of bright,
Heartbeats collide, igniting pure light.
In the cadence of longing, we find release,
A chorus of love that whispers its peace.

With every moment, we cultivate trust,
In this dance of heartbeats, fierce and just.
Together we navigate the path we start,
Guided forever by each other's heart.

Shards of Sunlight

Morning breaks with a brilliant glow,
Shards of sunlight on earth below.
Golden rays pierce the misty air,
Painting the world with a vibrant flair.

Each beam a promise, a warm caress,
Awakening life with tender finesse.
The flowers lift their heads in delight,
Dancing in joy, welcoming the light.

Sunlight dapples through leaves up high,
Creating patterns where shadows lie.
In every corner, a spark ignites,
Transforming the day, banishing blights.

As dusk approaches, the shards still gleam,
A reminder of warmth in twilight's dream.
Each fragment of sun, a memory bright,
Guiding us gently through the night.

Glimmers in the Gloom

In shadows cast by silent nights,
Faint whispers stir the hidden sights.
A flicker here, a glint of hope,
Where weary hearts learn how to cope.

Through darkened paths and heavy air,
A shimmer gleams, a light laid bare.
Amidst the weight of shadows cast,
We find the strength to hold on fast.

The stars above, a guiding sign,
They dance with dreams, both yours and mine.
In quiet corners, secrets bloom,
We find our peace, not lost in gloom.

With every dawn, a fresh new start,
Glimmers rise within the heart.
In life's embrace, we rise anew,
Together bright, we break on through.

Beacons of the Heart

In wandering paths where shadows play,
Beacons shine to light the way.
With gentle warmth and colors bright,
They lead us into love's sweet light.

Through valleys deep and mountains wide,
Hope's lantern flickers by our side.
Each pulse a rhythm, a guiding song,
Together we are, forever strong.

Through storms that rage and trials faced,
In every tear, we're not misplaced.
For in the depths, our hearts will find,
The beacons bright, to always bind.

Together forged in fire's embrace,
We shine with love, no time to waste.
With every beat, we chart our part,
United forever, beacons of the heart.

Fragments of Luminous Dreams

Shattered pieces of night's embrace,
Hold memories time cannot erase.
In every spark, a story glows,
Fragments dance where the wild wind blows.

In depths of silence, whispers call,
Dreams suspended, they rise and fall.
Each shimmering shard, a path unknown,
In twilight's weave, our fate is sown.

Through colors vast, in shadows deep,
We gather treasures that we keep.
A tapestry of hopes and schemes,
In broken pieces, we find our dreams.

With open hearts and steady hands,
We grasp the light where darkness stands.
In every fragment, visions gleam,
Together we create our dream.

Rays Beyond the Horizon

The sun spills gold on morning's dew,
A promise born, both bright and new.
With every breath, the world awakes,
As soft light dances on the lakes.

In whispers soft, the breezes sing,
Of hope bestowed, of life's sweet spring.
Each ray a brush to paint the sky,
As dreams take flight and spirits fly.

Across the vast and endless blue,
There lies a path, a journey true.
With open arms and hearts that soar,
We find our strength, we seek for more.

Together we'll chase the dawn's embrace,
With courage found, we'll set the pace.
In rays of light, we'll find our way,
Beyond the horizon, come what may.

Flickers of Eternal Joy

In the garden where sunlight falls,
Whispers of laughter lightly call,
Petals dance in the gentle breeze,
Moments captured, hearts at ease.

Stars appear as day takes flight,
Every glow a guiding light,
Time stands still, love's sweet embrace,
Flickers of joy in a sacred space.

With every breath, the world anew,
Dreams take shape, visions in view,
Hand in hand, we carve our way,
Eternal joy in each new day.

Through the shadows, hope will shine,
Like distant bells, our spirits align,
Flickers bright, they will not fade,
Together forever, love's crusade.

The Soft Illumination of Tomorrow

A dawn unfolds with tender grace,
Soft colors wrap the world's embrace,
Gentle breezes carry dreams,
Tomorrow glows with golden beams.

In the quiet moments, eyes awake,
Every heartbeat, a chance to take,
Whispers of hope invite us near,
Illumination that dries our tears.

Paths untraveled, stories untold,
Moments shared, both young and old,
With every step, new light will show,
Tomorrow's promise begins to grow.

As light expands, shadows retreat,
Each dawn a rhythm, a heart's heartbeat,
In the soft glow, we find our way,
Illumination guides us to stay.

A Symphony of Glimmers

Each raindrop falls in rhythmic song,
A symphony where hearts belong,
Melodies weave through the trees,
Nature hums with gentle ease.

In the twilight, colors blend,
Whispers of night, the day will end,
Stars like notes in the vast expanse,
Glimmers twirl in a cosmic dance.

Echoes gather, the silence speaks,
Harmony found in the soft peaks,
Together we rise, together we fall,
A symphony that unites us all.

With every glance and every sigh,
The world awakens beneath the sky,
Glimmers spark in the heart's warm embrace,
A symphony of love, a timeless grace.

Celestial Threads Unraveled

In the night sky, dreams take flight,
Stars like jewels, shining bright,
Threads of fate woven with care,
Celestial patterns, forever rare.

Galaxies whisper ancient lore,
Mysteries waiting to be explored,
Wonders join across endless space,
Unraveling time in a soft embrace.

With every heartbeat, the cosmos sighs,
Infinite wisdom in the starlit skies,
We are but threads in a grand design,
Celestial journeys, truly divine.

As we wander through the night,
Holding onto dreams, we find our light,
With each step, the path is clear,
Unraveled threads bring the stars near.

Silhouettes of Serenity

In twilight's gentle embrace,
Soft whispers float on air.
Nature's calm, a sacred space,
Where dreams and silence share.

Soft silhouettes in twilight glow,
Echoes of the day now fade.
Beneath the boughs, the cool winds blow,
As dusk's sweet peace invades.

The stars awaken, one by one,
Painting night with silver light.
In the stillness, hearts are won,
By the magic of the night.

In shadows deep, we find our rest,
With every breath, a lullaby.
In this haven, we are blessed,
As time slips softly by.

Dancing Shadows at Dawn

As dawn breaks with a tender hue,
Shadows stretch and softly sway.
Light dances with the morning dew,
Chasing night and dreams away.

The trees become a gentle stage,
Where whispers of the night retreat.
In this world, no thoughts of age,
Just rhythm of the heart's own beat.

Birds take flight, a fleeting song,
The sun awakens, bold and bright.
In every shadow, we belong,
As day unfolds in pure delight.

With each beam, the colors blend,
The earth ignites with joyous glee.
In this dance, we find a friend,
Embracing life's serenity.

Threads of Radiance

Through morning mist, the threads unwind,
Each golden ray, a story shared.
Weaving dreams of every kind,
In nature's tapestry, we're bared.

With every stitch of sunshine bright,
The world awakens, colors gleam.
In each moment, pure delight,
Life unfolds, a vibrant dream.

The gentle touch of light's embrace,
Fills the heart with warmth and grace.
Through woven paths, we find our place,
In this dance, we leave a trace.

As twilight draws its curtain close,
Stars emerge, a cosmic thread.
In every glow, our spirit grows,
In night's embrace, we lay our head.

Illuminated Whispers

In the silence, whispers hum,
Glowing softly in the night.
Through shadows deep, they gently come,
Guiding us with tender light.

Every secret, every sigh,
Twinkling like the twilight stars.
With open hearts, we learn to fly,
Embracing dreams that heal our scars.

The moon reflects our hidden pains,
Healing only time can mend.
Through illuminated lanes,
We grow strong, and hearts ascend.

In the echoes of the night,
Whispers dance upon the breeze.
Finding solace, we take flight,
As our spirits interweave.

Milton Keynes UK
Ingram Content Group UK Ltd.
UKHW020047181024
449757UK00011B/562